CHORAL FOLK SONGS FROM SOUTH AFRICA

INTRODUCTORY NOTES AND ENGLISH LYRICS BY PETE SEEGER

EDITED BY ROBERT DeCORMIER

ARRANGEMENTS TRANSCRIBED FROM AFRICAN PART SINGING BY REV. H. C. N. WILLIAMS AND J. N. MASELWA

CONTENTS

** New song in this edition*

FOREWORD

In all of New York City in 1952, there seemed to be only two South Africans, Prof. Z.K. Mathews at Union Theological Seminary, and his wife. He was too busy to see me, but his wife graciously answered my questions for several hours. She said she had heard my record of *Mbube,* which I called "Wimoweh," and she looked at some of the other 78rpm commercial recordings given to me at the same time by folklorist Alan Lomax, who was working at the time at Decca Recording Company (1949).

"These are all city songs," said Mrs. Mathews. "You should learn some of our older village songs, which are dying out as people have to go to the big cities to get jobs. At the missionary college where my husband used to teach, some students put on a whole evening of village songs. They were so well received that the little college published a songbook of them. I brought two copies to the United States. One copy I gave to the Schomburg Library in Harlem. The other I give to you."

The book was in "Tonic Sol Fa" notation, a style of music writing that missionaries spread over the world. *Drm* stands for *do, re, mi,* and various punctuation marks give the time value of the notes. I got a book explaining it, and over a month or so, I translated all these songs into the music notation most of us are used to. That summer I made up a bedtime story for my two small children, using the Xhosa lullaby "Abiyoyo." Two years later with some teenagers I recorded ten of the songs for tiny Folkways Records in New York City. I sent a copy of the LP to Hugh Tracey of the African Music Society, who played it for an African friend. He was a little contemptuous. "They're singing a Suto song with a Pondo ending," he said. We were not "authentic."

But, for twenty years I sang at least two of the songs for and with my college audiences. I'd get them singing "Bayeza ku-sa-sa bayeza" in three part harmony, over and over. Then I'd shout the high notes: "Oo-no-mo-tho-tho-la! E-ku-sen-i-na!" (See page 14).

"Somagwaza" haunts me even today. It's one of the most superb pieces of contrapuntal music in the entire world. In the key of A major I'd get half the audience, whether 50 or 5000, to memorize and sing the short bass part over and over. Then I'd get the other half to memorize and sing over and over the short high part. (Note that the word *somagwaza* ends the bass part, but it starts the high part). Each part would sing the word simultaneously. So, the whole audience would now be singing together, over and over and over, those six short measures. Before they would get bored with it, I then, with the microphone to help me, would sing the third part, which starts high, but ends in the middle range. After a minute, the song ends grandly with everyone singing "Somagwaza" in harmony. My friends and I have occasionally tried writing similar "cyclical" songs. None have ever even equaled "Somagwaza."

Well, now you have the book in your hands, and you can make up your own mind. In the huge continent of Africa, the cradle of the human race, there are hundreds of different languages, hundreds of different instruments, many different types of melody, and different types of antiphony–gospel churches call it "answer-back" or "call and response." The people of South Africa especially like to sing in rich harmony. Three parts, four parts, five parts, six parts or more. Here's wishing you good luck as you explore for yourself!

~Pete Seeger

P.S. 50% of the royalties for the "Abiyoyo" story go to the Ubuntu Education Fund.

Ubuntu Education Fund
32 Broadway, Suite 414, New York, NY 10004
(646) 827-1190, info@ubuntufund.org, www.ubuntufund.org

Ubuntu sends the money directly to the committee for libraries and scholarships near Port Elizabeth and Durban in Southeastern South Africa, where the lullaby originated... how many years ago, no one knows. This is part of the Campaign for Public Domain Reform, which started 15 years ago in New York. You can learn more about it from the WIPO (World Intellectual Property-Rights Organization) office in Geneva, Switzerland. If any reader composes new words to the music in this book, and records them, they can contact Ubuntu, which also means "share" in the Xhosa language.

I first became familiar with *Choral Folk Songs from South Africa* when Pete Seeger and a group of teenagers, called the Song Swappers, recorded some of these songs for Folkways Records in 1955. One of the Song Swappers was Mary Travers, who later became the "Mary" of Peter, Paul and Mary.

I was pleased, when, a few years later, G. Schirmer published a collection of these songs. When they first appeared there was very little available of this wonderful African choral music. The book made it possible for choral directors and song leaders to acquaint their singers with music of a culture we knew little or nothing about.

The music can be adapted and used with young children, as well as high school and adult singers. For the most part, the language is very manageable, with the exception of the "click" consonants, which will require a fair amount of practice. In addition, Pete has created excellent singing English translations for some of these songs.

For a long time, this collection had been out of print. I am overjoyed that it is once again available. I hope that you find it both as useful and enjoyable as I have.

~Robert DeCormier

PRONUNCIATION GUIDE

VOWELS:

A = *ah*
E = as in *egg* or *obey*
I = *ee* as in *seek*
O = *oh* or *aw*
U = *oo* as in *oo-la-la*

CONSONANTS:

As written, and every one is pronounced. Two exceptions:

ph as in *peanut*, not *phone*
hl as in *hluluwe*
(keep front tip of tongue against palate while making a *sh* sound, but not *shlushluwe*)

Many South African words have what are called "clicks":

X = Sideways click (as in spurring a horse).
Press the tongue against the upper inside of teeth and pull it away rapidly, sucking in as to say, "giddyup"
Example: *isiXhosa AmaXhosa uxola*

C = Tongue in front
Press the tip of the tongue against the upper front teeth and rapidly pull it away, as to say, "tut, tut" or "tsk, tsk"
Example: *Nceda ndcela kancinci*

Q = Tongue in middle (cork popping/door knocking)
Press the front part of the tongue against the hard palate behind the front teeth and rapidly pull it away.
Example: *Qo nkqo*

Agglutination: Xhosa is a "glutinous" language, meaning that vowels at the beginning and end of words are often swallowed, words or syllables thus becoming "glued" together.

FROM THE EDITOR:

I wish to express my gratitude to Melissa Chesnut-Tangerman for her help with translations and pronunciation, and to Nathaniel G. Lew for transcribing the four new songs from tonic "sol-fa" to our traditional notation, and to South Africans, Craig Charnock and Dr. Benjamin Locke of Kenyan College for their generous help.

~Robert DeCormier

INTRODUCTION

[Ed. note: This Introduction is adapted from the 1960 edition.]

What does the average American think of when he hears the word Africa? Most of us know very little about the traditions of this great continent. Tremendous civilizations there were destroyed by centuries of the slave trade and wars of conquest. Over two thousand years ago they were forging iron and casting brass, at a time when men in Northern Europe were still using stone hatchets. Eight hundred years ago a university flourished at Timbuktu, drawing scholars from many lands to its halls. Today, one can find African cultural expressions which challenge the world to produce their equal for beauty, vigor, subtlety and rich variety. Music is one of these.

The music of Africa has become justly famous for its complex and exciting rhythms, but the great variety of other music indigenous to that continent is not so generally known. For example, in East Africa one can find large xylophone orchestras; in West Africa the predecessor of the American banjo is still played. Flutes, trumpets, bowed instruments, thumb pianos and harps are used for playing traditional music, as well as contemporary music influenced by European techniques and styles.

In Southern Africa, choral music has long been a favorite. The first European explorers heard village choruses singing rich harmonies, with counterpoint and antiphony entirely African in character.

The songs in this collection are not of this ancient type, neither are they the jazzy songs now popular in large cities like Johannesburg. They are what may be heard today in the small villages of Capetown Province and show the influence of over one hundred and fifty years of contact with European conquerors and missionaries. For example, "Here's to the Couple" shows a great deal of missionary influence; however, "Somagwaza" shows practically none.

The vocal arrangements are printed almost exactly as sung by a group of African students in Capetown Province in 1947. Their concert was so successful that a book of the songs was printed. We quote from the editors' preface to the first edition.

"…This book is the result of five students of St. Matthews College, members of a choir of eight which broadcast a series of programs of African Folk Songs for the South African Broadcasting Corporation. The five students are Khulukazi Mptai, Norauti Klass, Joseph Maselwa, Alfred Mangcu and Sabelo Mjali.

Many have heard Africans singing, and have been impressed with the resonance of the harmonies and the attractiveness of the rhythms, but few have ever regarded these harmonies and rhythmic effects as songs with a clear melody, and still fewer have felt them to be beautiful music representative of a unique and valuable tradition. Prejudice based on ignorance of the music which these songs represent and an undue exaggeration of the lack of 'respectability' in their associations in non-Christian customs have been responsible for their rapid disappearance…

CHORAL FOLK SONGS FROM SOUTH AFRICA

The present arrangement of these songs does not pretend to be final, and indeed it is to be very much hoped that those using this book will use their imagination and make their own arrangements of these songs. Where possible, the characteristic and beautiful polyphony of some of the songs has been brought out in the form of rounds. Others, such as the lullabies, lend themselves to acted games for the very young. Others, such as "Oonomot'hot'holo" suggest song games for children.

No formal notation can convey the intricacies of rhythm and suspended syncopation. Perhaps it would have been better to print them without bars, but this would assume that readers and singers would know the time of each song; whereas, many will never have heard the songs at all. It must, however, be strongly emphasized that these bars and note values are only intended as a preliminary guide, and every encouragement should be given to freedom of expression to keep the natural rhythmic flow essential to the attractiveness of the songs.

Great difficulty has been experienced as a result of the impossibility of conveying the times of the songs as heard, to the formal settings of this book... This is accounted for largely by the recitative effect of disregarding the normal time for two or three bars to crowd in additional words, while the time is 'assumed', and then of returning to strict time values for the completion of the phrase. This is a very characteristic form. A further complication is presented by the fact that in many of the songs as heard, the Cantor or 'Umhlabeli' adds a flowing descant which often bears no direct relation to the time of the remaining parts."

H.C.N. Williams
J.N. Maselwa
St. Matthews College, January, 1947

We need add only a few words to the American who will pick up this slim volume and try to sing some of the songs in it. First, regard them as you would any folk song, to be sung for the enjoyment of it, with an open, unaffected tone of voice. Many are cyclical songs like rounds, which may be repeated almost endlessly.

Second, while we would want to be faithful to the original spirit of the songs, we should frankly admit that we cannot duplicate exactly the way they are sung in Africa. For one thing, African scales have not the same pitch relationships as our major and minor scales, and our voices are unused to traditional African inflections, slides and accents. But there is much of Africa already in American folk traditions, and these songs can be learned very quickly by anyone familiar with spirituals, blues and square dances.

These wonderful songs are meant to be sung, and should not be treated as museum pieces. There is no reason why African folk songs should not be added to the world's heritage of song. In time we may come to sing them as we do "Auld Lang Syne" or "Silent Night," without bothering to make a big point about the country of their origin.

It may be of interest to listen to the Folkways LP recording *Bantu Folk Songs* [Ed. note: now available on CD through www.folkways.si.edu as Folkways Records FW06912] to see what a chorus composed mainly of New York high school students did with these songs. Banjo and guitar accompaniment was added. Incidentally, these instruments are quite common in South African towns today.

For the record, let us note here precisely what few changes have been made for this American edition:

Chord indications, for guitar, banjo or some other folk instrument, have been given in a few songs. While not absolutely necessary, such accompaniment will make the songs much easier to teach. In South Africa such Western instruments are now well known, although traditionally these songs would more often be accompanied by clapping, rattles or hand drums.

In a few of the songs, the original keys have been changed, usually by bringing the melodies down to a range more comfortable for average voices. This has necessitated the occasional alteration of a few bass notes.

The most obvious change is, of course, the addition of English lyrics. Wherever possible, we urge singers to attempt the original African words (which are in several different languages, such as Pondo, Xhosa, Sutho, etc.). Where the words seem too difficult, English lyrics have been composed which keep to the subject matter, but do not pretend to be a direct translation. Poetic translation is one of the most difficult of literary tasks; in the case of songs, it is almost impossible to find suitable meanings coupled with singable sounds.

Even in translation, many of the African lyrics would still be meaningless. Mr. Henry Ramaila, when he was a student at the Union Theological Seminary, was able to translate most of the songs, but gave up on many. "This song is untranslatable; it is felt by Africans," he noted under "Somagwaza." Of "Manamolela" he said; "Don't try to render this song in English. It will make no sense. The idiom has no equivalent to give the exact emotion in English."

So let us not be surprised if through the years new words get composed for many of these melodies. It will do no injustice to the magnificent folk traditions of a great continent, and can only serve to strengthen the bonds of friendship between peoples.

How representative are these songs of African folk music? The music in this collection is typical of one small corner of that vast continent, the villages of South Africa, mainly Capetown Province, in a particular period of their history, midway between a tribal past and a cosmopolitan future. The English lyrics are, in the main, different in meaning from the African original and represent a grafting on of a new stalk to the original plant.

For more information on African music we refer you to the recent LPs put out by such recording companies as London, Columbia, Folkways[1], Riverside and others. An excellent short book introducing the basic principles of African music is *Ngoma*[2] by Hugh Tracey, Secretary of the African Music Society (published by Longmans Green, New York, London).

We wish to express our thanks to Mr. Ramaila for the translations, and to Mrs. Z. K. Mathews for introducing the original collection to us. Special thanks go to Rev. Williams and Mr. Maselwa, editors of the collection, and to Lovedale Missionary College, the owner of the book's original copyright. Most especially, thanks to the peoples of South Africa, who created these works of art through the centuries, and have passed them on to us.

~Pete Seeger

Ed. notes:

[1]*Bantu Choral Folksongs,* an LP record originally issued by Folkways Recordings, is now available on CD through Smithsonian Folkways Recordings: www.folkways.si.edu.

[2]*Ngoma* is now out of print, but may be available in libraries or from used book dealers.

Photo: Anthony Pepitone

Pete Seeger has been integral in the advancement of the preservation and recognition of folk music. His passion for politics, the environment and humanity is the subject of the documentary, *Pete Seeger: The Power of Song.* He is a member of both the Songwriters' and Rock and Roll Halls of Fame, and is the recipient of such awards as the Kennedy Center Lifetime Achievement Honor and the National Medal of Arts. He has recorded over 100 albums and has authored the book *Where Have All the Flowers Gone?: A Musical Autobiography.* It is his hope that the songs included in this book will be shared with young people throughout the world.

Robert DeCormier is a graduate of the Juilliard School of Music. His conducting engagements have taken him from Broadway and opera to the Berkshire Choral Institute, the Zimriya World Assembly of Choirs in Israel and numerous concert tours throughout the United States and Canada with his own professional group, the Robert DeCormier Singers. He spent many years as music director of the New York Choral Society. In addition, he has served as conductor and arranger for Harry Belafonte and has been music director for the popular folk trio, Peter, Paul and Mary, for the past 20 years. His composition list is extensive, ranging from choral to ballet to Broadway scores, as well as recording and television credits. Mr. DeCormier resides in Belmont, Vermont and now directs Counterpoint, a professional vocal ensemble.

LULLABIES

1. ABIYOYO
Lullaby

This lullaby comes at the conclusion of a bedtime story in which a monster threatens little children. The children are given a charm for their protection, which inspires them to sing this song. The rhythm affects the monster so powerfully that he is induced to dance. In this state of emotion he is quickly dispensed with by the fathers and mothers of the children.

No English lyric is needed for this song, since the melody was originally sung to only the one word. It should be sung over and over until the child is asleep.

Chord indications have been given for some simple instrument such as a guitar, but accompaniment is not really necessary, as should be kept to a minimum.

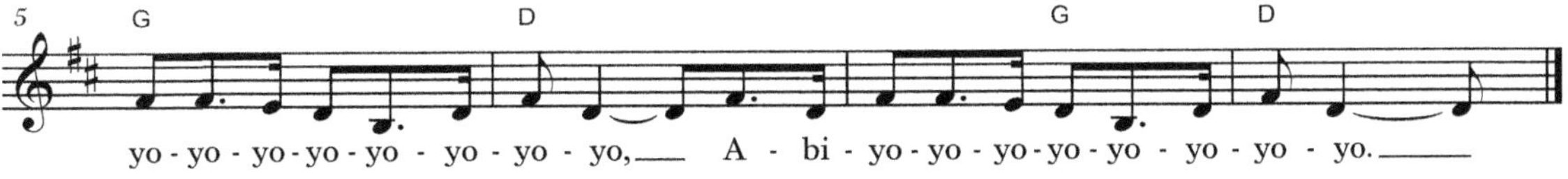

CHORAL FOLK SONGS FROM SOUTH AFRICA

2. HEY, T'HOLA, T'HOLA
Lullaby

This song might be sung by the eldest daughter of the house, as she rocks the youngest child to sleep. The men of the house join in a soft refrain.

A literal translation of the African words is: *Be silent, my child.* The words then go on to recall the grazing of horses in the melon fields during the day. The English lyrics are not an exact translation, but, it is hoped, carry out the original feeling.

Note: The bass and tenor parts must not be allowed to outweigh the melody, which must be sung *pianissimo.*

T'hola, t'hola ngoaname; t'hola, t'hola, ngoaname
Li pere sera peng' Rapeng sama hapu
Eitsa li lo tsela tsa ea ngoaname
Ei, eingoaname,

Ei, eingoaname,
Ha le so bone donkoti, ha le so bone kontoki,
T'hola, t'hola ngoaname
T'hola, t'hola ngoaname

Hush-a, hush-a my baby; hush-a, hush-a my baby,
Hush, never mind the wind blowing through the trees.
Once on a time was a young little lion,
Took him to the doctor to make him mind me.
Ah-ee, hush-a my baby,
Ae-ee, hush-a my baby.
Once on a time a dove, sitting in a tree above, sang
"T'hola, t'hola," he sang to me.
"T'hola, t'hola," he sang to me.

PRONUNCIATION:
i = ee
e as in *egg; ea = eh-ah*
u as in *lute*
a as in *father*
t'h is a cross between *t* and *th*
ngoa = ngwa

2. HEY, T'HOLA, T'HOLA
Lullaby

CHORAL FOLK SONGS FROM SOUTH AFRICA

Ha le so bone kon ko - ti, ha le so bone kon - ko - ti,
Once on a time a dove sit - ting in a tree a - bove sang
Ha le so bone kon - ko - ti, ha le so bone kon - ko - ti,
Once on a time a dove sit - ting in a tree a - bove sang
Hey, t'ho - la t'ho - la, hey, t'ho - la t'ho - la,
Hey, t'ho - la t'ho - la, hey, t'ho - la t'ho - la,
T'ho - la, t'ho-la ngoa-na - me, T'ho - la, t'ho-la ngoa-na - me.
"T'ho - la, t'ho-la" he sang me; "T'ho - la, t'ho-la" he sang to me.
T'ho - la, t'ho-la ngoa-na - me, T'ho - la, t'ho-la ngoa-na - me.
"T'ho - la, t'ho-la" he sang me; "T'ho - la, t'ho-la" he sang to me.
Hey, t'ho-la t'ho - la, hey t'ho-la t'ho - la.
Hey, t'ho-la t'ho - la, hey t'ho-la t'ho - la.

WORK SONGS

3. MANAMOLELA
Work Song

This Sutho song is sung during hoeing. It is a song of weariness, in which the singers beg their employer to be relieved.

Literally translated the words mean: *Mediator (foreman), O Mediator, behold, we are tired; alas, we are tired.* However, in a fundamental sense, the idiom has no exact emotional equivalent in English. Try to use the word "foreman"; we have left the African word *Manomolela* in the English lyrics.

Manamolela, manamolela
Won't you let us take it slow?
Won't you let us take it slow?
You know the day is long,
You know the day is long.
Manamolela, manamolela
Helele re khat'hetsi
Helele re khat'hetsi
Ahere khat'hetsi!

PRONUNCIATION:
i = ee
e as in *egg*
u as in *lute*
a as in *father*
kh like the *ch* in *Bach*
t'h is a cross between *t* and *th*

3. MANAMOLELA
Work Song

CHORAL FOLK SONGS FROM SOUTH AFRICA

13
Ma - na - mo - le - la, Ma - na - mo - le -
Ma - na - mo - le - la, Ma - na - mo - le -
kha - t'he - tsi   He - le - le - re   kha - t'he - tsi   He - le - le - re
day is long.   Won't you let us   take it slow?   Won't you let us
17
la, He - le - le - re kha - t'he - tsi,   He - le - le re kha - t'he - tsi
la, Won't you let us take it slow?   Won't you let us take it slow?
kha - t'he - tsi   A - he - re kha - t'he - tsi   A - he - re
take it slow?   You know the day is long,   You know the
21
A - he - re kha - t'he - tsi,   A - he - re kha - t'he - tsi!
You know the day is long,   You know the day is long.
kha - t'he - tsi.
day is long.

4. BAYANDOYIKA
Work Song

This song is frequently sung by girls whenever they do work of any sort in company. Thus it is often heard during hoeing, stamping of mealies, carrying water from the river, or gathering wood. A literal translation of the words is: *They fear me, O the children of heathen.*

One can see the difficulty of making suitable English lyrics.

We have transposed the soprano part (the lead) for tenor, and given an alto part to the bass. The original key of B-flat has been changed to D. No other changes in words or music have been made.

All the parts do not have to start at the same time. It is actually more characteristic if they enter gradually, one by one. Then the song is repeated, like a round, until the singers finally grow weary.

There is one tricky bit of pronunciation to observe. The letters *gq* represent a clucking noise, made by pulling the tongue down from the back part of the roof of the mouth. It is a sound difficult for Americans to make, but not impossible. In the Folkways record FP60A *Millions of Musicians,* [Ed. note: Available on CD from www.folkways.si.edu, FW05560] one can hear a South African woman pronounce a tongue-twister full of such clicks. It is a feature of language believed to have been picked up from neighboring Khoe-San tribes.

The sharpened 4th note of the scale, G-sharp, might sound strange to our ears, but is actually quite common in some parts of Africa. Perhaps it is worth remembering that many African-American folk songs tend not only to flatten the 3rd and 7th notes of the major scale, but also to sharpen the 4th.

Ewe, bayandoyika bantwan', Ewe nomama, bayandoyika bantwan',
Bayandoyika bantwanabama gqo boka

PRONUNCIATION:
e as in *egg* (*Ewe* sounds almost like *away*.)
a as in *father*
i like *ee*
gq is a click (see above)

4. BAYANDOYIKA
Work Song

5. INKOSI YAMAMPONDO
Work Song

This song is normally sung during any work by boys in company, though it is properly a song sung by herd boys when they drive the cattle, sheep and goats home in the evening.

TRANSLATION:
inkosi – lord or chief
Amampondo – one of the tribes that makes up the Xhosa
iyabaleka – he is running
Yabakwetha – of the Abakweta

The remaining words are basically nonsense syllables.

5. INKOSI YAMAMPONDO
Work Song

CHORAL FOLK SONGS FROM SOUTH AFRICA

SONGS TO ACCOMPANY SPECIFIC CEREMONIES

In America, certain songs, (Christmas songs, "Happy Birthday to You," etc.) are closely connected with specific occasions. The following five songs are closely connected with certain African village ceremonies. If the melodies seem to repeat themselves almost endlessly, realize that they might be more like a choral accompaniment to a dance, rather than a "song" as we know it. The dance might be extremely syncopated and complicated, so the song would intentionally be kept simple.

6. BAYEZA (Oonomot'hot'holo)
Ceremonial Song

The craft of the African shaman is built around a number of spirits, each with its own particular function. One of the more mischievous of these is the Nomothotholo, which, among other doubtful habits, hovers over the chimney tops of houses, and reports any useful conversation to the shaman, and is not above running down the chimney from time to time to steal tobacco if it is left lying about. This song is an invocation to this spirit to come with the dawn.

This song is one of the simplest to learn, and can be taught to an audience and sung in three- or four-part harmony within a few minutes. It is printed here in the exact arrangement transcribed in Africa. It becomes quite effective when parts are gradually added and then taken away. There is no need for English lyrics, since the few African words are so easily pronounced.

Oonomot'hot'holo! Eku senina!
Oonomot'hot'holo bayeza kusasa
Bayeza kusasa bayeza
Bayeza kusasa bayeza

PRONUNCIATION:
oo = loon
o as in *obey*
e as in *egg*
i like *ee*
kh like the *ch* in *Bach*
t'h is a cross between *t* and *th*

6. BAYEZA (Oonomot'hot'holo)
Ceremonial Song

CHORAL FOLK SONGS FROM SOUTH AFRICA

CHORAL FOLK SONGS FROM SOUTH AFRICA

sa - sa. Oo-no-mo - t'ho-t'ho-lo ba - ye - za ku - sa - sa. Oo-no-mo-
sa-sa, ba-ye - za, ba-ye - za, ku - sa-sa, ba-ye - za,
sa-sa, ba-ye - za, ba-ye - za, ku - sa-sa, ba-ye - za,
sa-sa, ba-ye - za, ba-ye - za, ku - sa-sa, ba-ye - za,
ho, ho-no-ma - ha, Ha, ho, ho, ho-no-ma - ha,
t'ho-t'ho-lo! E - ku se-ni-na. Oo-no-mo - t'ho-t'ho-lo! E - ku-
ba - ye - za, ku - sa - sa, ba-ye - za, ba-ye - za, ku-
ba - ye - za, ku - sa - sa, ba-ye - za, ba-ye - za, ku-
ba - ye - za, ku - sa - sa, ba-ye - za, ba-ye - za, ku-
Ha, ho, ho, ho-no-ma - ha, ha, ho,
Ba-ye - za, ku - sa - sa, ba-ye - za, ba-ye - za, ku-
mf

se - ni - a. Oo - no - mo - t'ho - t'ho - lo, ba - ye - za, ku - sa - sa. Oo - no - mo -
sa - sa, ba - ye - za, ba - ye - za, ku - sa - sa, ba - ye - za,
sa - sa, ba - ye - za, ba - ye - za, ku - sa - sa, ba - ye - za,
sa - sa, ba - ye - za, ba - ye - za, ku - sa - sa, ba - ye - za,
ho, ho - no - ma - ha, ha, ho, ho, ho - no - ma - ha,
sa - sa, ba - ye - za, ba - ye - za, ku - sa - sa, ba - ye - za,
t'ho - t'ho - lo, ba - ye - za ku - sa - sa. Oo - no - mo t'ho - t'ho - lo! E - ku -
ba - ye - za, ku - sa - sa, ba - ye - za, ba - ye - za, ku -
ba - ye - za, ku - sa - sa, ba - ye - za, ba - ye - za, ku -
ba - ye - za, ku - sa - sa, ba - ye - za, ba - ye - za, ku -
ha, ho, ho, ho - no - ma - ha, ha, ho,
ba - ye - za, ku - sa - sa, ba - ye - za, ba - ye - za, ku -

se - ni - a. Oo-no-mo - t'ho-t'ho-lo! E - ku - se-ni - a. Oo-no-mo-
sa - sa, ba-ye - za, ba-ye - za, ku - sa-sa, ba-ye - za,
sa - sa, ba-ye - za, ba-ye - za, ku - sa-sa, ba-ye - za,
sa - sa, ba-ye - za, ba-ye - za, ku - sa-sa, ba-ye - za,
ho, ho-no-ma - ha, ha, ho, ho, ho-no-ma - ha,
sa - sa, ba-ye - za,
poco a poco dim.
t'ho-t'ho-lo ba-ye-za ku - sa - sa. Oo-no-mo - t'ho-t'ho-lo ba-ye-za ku
poco a poco dim.
ba-ye - za, ku - sa-sa, ba-ye - za, ba-ye - za, ku -
poco a poco dim.
ba-ye - za, ku - sa-sa, ba-ye - za, ba-ye - za, ku -
poco a poco dim.
ba-ye - za, ku - sa-sa, ba-ye - za, ba-ye - za, ku -
poco a poco dim.
ha, ho, ho, ho-no-ma - ha.
poco a poco dim.

sa - sa. Oo - no - mo - t'ho-t'ho-lo! E - ku se - ni - na. Oo-no-mo-
sa-sa, ba-ye - za, ba-ye - za, ku - sa - sa, ba-ye - za,
sa-sa, ba-ye - za, ba-ye - za, ku - sa - sa, ba-ye - za,
sa-sa, ba-ye - za, ba-ye - za, ku - sa - sa, ba-ye - za.
t'ho-t'ho-lo! E - ku - se-ni-a. Oo-no-mo - t'ho-t'ho-lo ba-ye - za ku
ba-ye - za, ku - sa - sa, ba-ye - za, ba-ye - za, ku-
ba-ye - za, ku - sa - sa, ba-ye - za, ba-ye - za, ku-

sa-sa. Oo-no-mo - t'ho-t'ho-lo! Oo-no-mo-t'ho-t'ho-lo! Oo-no-mo-
sa-sa, ba-ye - za.
sa-sa, ba-ye - za.
t'ho-t'ho-lo ba - ye-za ku-sa-sa. Oo-no-mo-t'ho-t'ho-lo ba-
Ba - ye - za, ku-sa-sa, ba-ye - za, ba-
Ba - ye - za, ku-sa-sa, ba-ye - za, ba-
Ba - ye - za, ku-sa-sa, ba-ye - za, ba-
Ha, ho, ho, ho-no - ma - ha,
Ba - ye - za, ku-sa-sa, ba-ye - za, ba-

ye - za ku - sa - sa. Oo - no - mo - t'ho - t'ho - lo ba -
ye - za, ku - sa - sa, ba - ye - za, ba -
ye - za, ku - sa - sa, ba - ye - za, ba -
ye - za, ku - sa - sa, ba - ye - za, ba -
ha, ho, ho, ho - no - ma - ha, ba -
ye - za, ku - sa - sa, ba - ye - za, ba -
ye - za ku - sa - sa, ba - ye - za.
ye - za, ku - sa - sa, ba - ye - za.
ye - za, ku - sa - sa, ba - ye - za.
ye - za, ku - sa - sa, ba - ye - za.
ye - za, ku - sa - sa, ba - ye - za.
ye - za, ku - sa - sa, ba - ye - za.

7. INGOMA YA BAKWETA
Ceremonial Song

During the period when the Abakweta are in their initiation huts, they may not openly visit the village. If they require anything from the village, they must communicate their requirements by song. In this song, they send a vocal message for meat. The girls who are sent to take the meat to them join in this song of the Abakweta.

7. INGOMA YA BAKWETA

Ceremonial Song

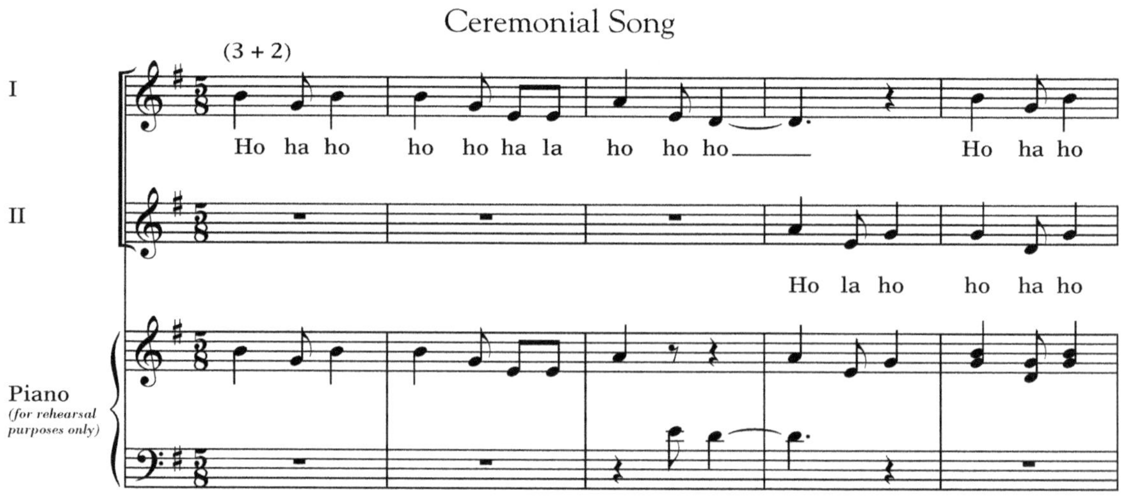

CHORAL FOLK SONGS FROM SOUTH AFRICA

8. SOMAGWAZA
Ceremonial Song

A most important ceremony in Africa, as in many other parts of the world, occurs when young men are initiated into manhood. The group of boys who have reached the required age live in a special house in the village, and are given a course of training equipping them for the duties of adult citizenship.

At the end of the Abakweta period of initiation the boys wash off the ceremonial clay from their bodies. They leave their huts on the hillside, and run down to the river to wash, singing this song as they go. The song is usually interrupted by various types of 'war cries' of the question and answer type.

Like other songs in this collection, no one vocal part is very complicated, but put together, the three voices achieve a subtle counter-rhythmic effect. With continued repetition, the sonority and rhythmic balance is perfected.

The translator, Mr. Ramaila, assures us that this song "...cannot be translated. It is felt by Africans." Whatever specific meaning the words once had has been lost. A similar situation occurs in America with many nursery rhymes.

Hawe, hawe somagwaza
Somagwaza mna yo weh, yo weh
Hey mna yo weh, hey mna yo weh, somagwaza

PRONUNCIATION:
e as in *egg*
a like *father* (*hawe* sounds almost like *hah-way*)
o as in *obey*

8. SOMAGWAZA

Ceremonial Song

CHORAL FOLK SONGS FROM SOUTH AFRICA

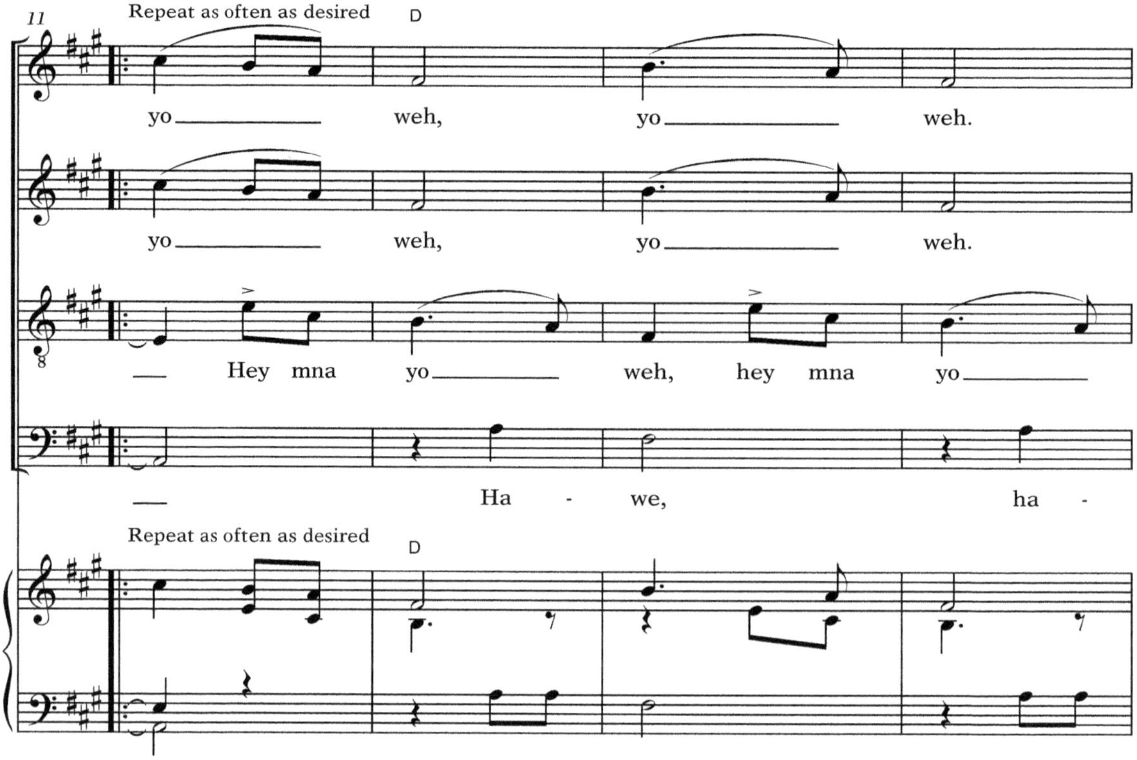

Repeat as often as desired
D
yo weh, yo weh.
yo weh, yo weh.
Hey mna yo weh, hey mna yo
Ha - we, ha -
Repeat as often as desired
D
All but last time
A
Last time
A rit.
So - ma - gwa - za mna So - ma - gwa - za.
So - ma - gwa - za mna So - ma - gwa - za.
rit.
weh, so - ma - gwa - za, weh, so - ma - gwa - za.
rit.
we so - ma - gwa - za, weh, so - ma - gwa - za.
rit.
All but last time
A
Last time
A

9. OALLA MOHOLOLI
Ceremonial Song

This Sutho song is sung when the boys return home after the initiation ceremony.

Oalla means literally: *It cries.* The words tell of a bird that senses a battle far off, and describes the slaughter that will take place.

Over half of the lyrics consist only of the two words in the title. These are easy and beautiful to pronounce. When the sopranos and altos come to the more difficult African words, they may simply sing: *La, la, la,* etc., or some such simple English phrases as given below. A literal translation would not only be unsingable and unpoetic, but would still not carry the proper meaning to non-Africans.

Oalla, oalla mohololi, oalla
Hololi mohololi!
Me oee, ntate oee!
Mafokotsane bo mali nakana
Ke t'ho tse kango anemotle li t'ha beng
Me oee, ntate oee!
Eea loan a e ea loan a makhafola
E loan a kali peke le li khara fu
Oalla, oalla.

Oalla, oalla mohololi! Oalla, oalla mohololi!
Hololi mohololi!
Look away, look away!
You hear the swallow calling, look away!
You hear the mountain calling, look away!
Look away, look away!
You hear the future calling, look away!
You hear the others calling, look away!

PRONUNCIATION:
i = ee
e as in *egg*
kh like the *ch* in *Bach*
u as in *lute*
o as in *obey*
oa is a rapid diphthong made while opening the lips to an *a*, as in *father*

9. OALLA MOHOLOLI
Ceremonial Song

CHORAL FOLK SONGS FROM SOUTH AFRICA

9
Me__ oee! nta-te oee! Me__ oee
Look a-way, look a-way. Look a-way,
oa - lla mo-ho-lo-li! Me__ oee! nta-te oee!
Look a-way, look a-way.
ho-lo-li! Ho-li-li mo-ho-lo-li!
Oa - lla, oa - lla, mo-ho-lo-li! Oa-lla,
12
nta - te oee! Ma - fo - ko-tsa - ne
look a - way! You hear the swal-low
Me__ oee nta - te oee!
Look a - way, look a - way!
Ho - li - li mo - ho - lo - li!
oa - lla, mo-ho-lo-li! Oa - lla,

14
bo ma - li na - ka - na._______ Ke t'ho tse kan - go
call - ing, look a - way._______ You hear the moun - tain
___ Ma - fo - ko - tsa - ne bo ma - li na - ka - na._______
___ You hear the swal - low call - ing, look a - way._______
___ Ho - li - li mo - ho - lo - li!_______
oa - lla, mo - ho - lo - li! Oa - lla,

16
ane - mo - tle li t'ha beng._______ Me ___ oee
call - ing, look a - way._______ Look a - way,
___ Ke t'ho tse kan - go ane - mo - tle li t'ha beng._
___ You hear the moun - tain call - ing, look a - way._
___ Ho - li - li mo - ho - lo - li!_______
oa - lla, mo - ho - lo - li! Oa - lla,

nta - te oee!
look a - way!
Me_ oee nta - te oee!
Look a - way, look a - way!
Me_ oee
Look a - way,
Me_ oee nta - te oee!
Look a - way, look a - way!
Me_ oee
Look a - way,
Ho - li - li mo - ho - lo - li!
Ho - li - li mo -
oa - lla, mo - ho - lo - li!
Oa - lla,
oa - lla, mo - ho - lo - li!
E - ea loa na e ea loa na ma kha fo la.
You hear the fu - ture call - ing, look a - way.
E loa na ka - li
You hear the oth - ers
nta - te oee!
look a - way!
E - ea loa na e ea loa na ma kha fo la.
You hear the fu - ture call - ing, look a - way.
ho - lo - li!
Ho - li - li mo - ho - lo - li!
Oa - lla,
oa - lla, mo - ho - lo - li!
Oa - lla,

pe - ke le li kha - ra fu.
call - ing, look a - way.

E loa na ka - li pe ke le li kha - ra fu.
You hear the oth - ers call - ing, look a - way.

Ho - li - li mo - ho - lo - li! Oa - lla, mo-ho-lo-li!
oa - lla, mo-ho-lo-li! Oa - lla, oa-lla, mo-ho-lo-li!

Oa - lla, oa - lla.
Oa - lla, oa - lla, oa - lla, oa - lla.

10. HEY, TSWANA
Ceremonial Song

This song is sung by the boys at the end of the initiation ceremony, when they reach their homes. The girls of the village join the *bashemane* (the initiates) in the song, which praises the boys for their achievements, which have become exaggerated in their minds during the weeks of initiation.

Again we find the words are so simple as to make translation superfluous. The song can start simply and end simply, with the voices gradually joining each other and gradually dropping out. Although we have indicated a possible guitar accompaniment, it is not necessary.

Hey tswana, nehe tipe same tswana
Hey tswana, nehe tipe same tswana

PRONUNCIATION:
a as in *father*
e as in *egg*
i like *ee* (*same* tends to sound like *sah-may*)

10. HEY, TSWANA

Ceremonial Song

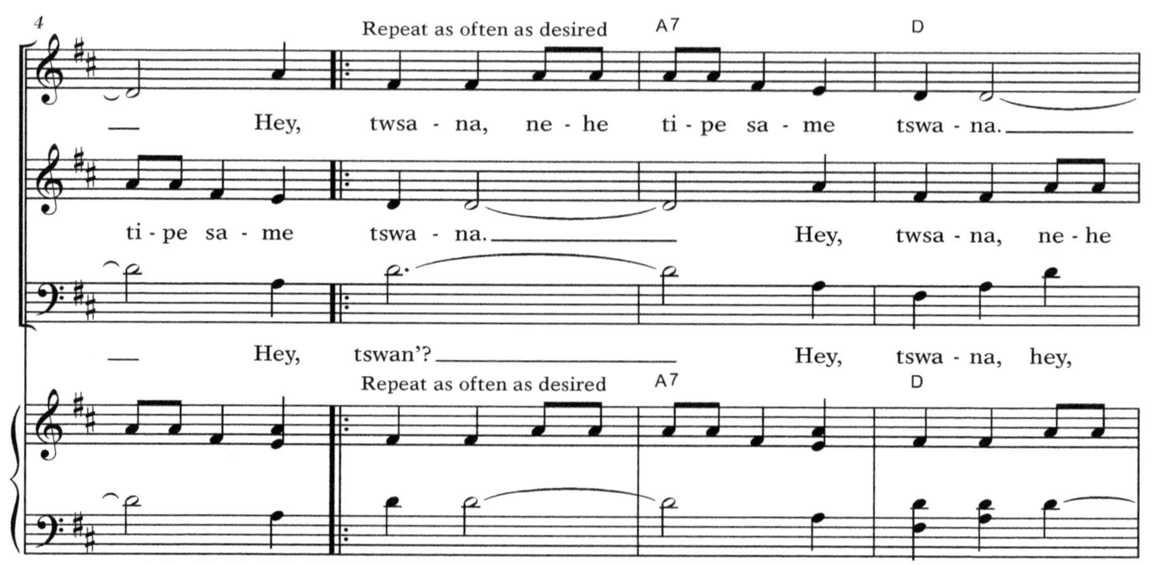

CHORAL FOLK SONGS FROM SOUTH AFRICA

CHORAL FOLK SONGS FROM SOUTH AFRICA

WEDDING SONGS

A delightful, neighborly custom is followed in the villages of South Africa. When a young couple is married, friends of the bride form a chorus, and friends of the groom form a chorus. A "singing competition" between the two groups is held intermittently during the days and nights of the celebration. Today, the prescribed formalities are often a combination of ancient pagan customs and Christian regulations introduced by the missionaries. Thus the words of most of the songs in this section are of comparatively recent origin, while the tunes are apt to be much older. However, some of the melodies tend to be more Western than some of the preceding songs.

11. VUL'EMNYANGO
Wedding Song

On the eve of the wedding, the bridegroom's party arrives at the home of the bride, and is given a room in which to spend the night. After dark, the "singing contest" is begun by the bridegroom's party visiting the hut in which the singers of the bride's party are waiting to be formally told of the arrival of the visitors. They do this by "knocking at the door" – only they do not knock physically, but by singing this song.

Nkgo, nkgo nkgo.
Nkgo, nkgo, nkgo.
Nkgo, nkgo, nkgo, vul'emnyango shu, shu, shu kuyabanda.
Yitshoni nonke, yitshoni nonke sigalelekile.

Knock, knock, knock.
Knock, knock, knock, oh, won't you open the door, the wind blows cold.
Knock, knock, knock, oh, please come open the door, the wind blows cold.
Come open the door, the rain is pouring down.

11. VUL'EMNYANGO
Wedding Song
English lyric by
Louise Dobbs
♩ = ca. 120
Arranged by
Robert DeCormier
Soprano
Alto
Tenor
Bass
Piano
(for rehearsal purposes only)
♩ = ca. 120
Nkgo, nkgo, nkgo. Nkgo, nkgo, nkgo. Nkgo, nkgo,
Nkgo, nkgo, nkgo. Nkgo, nkgo, nkgo. Nkgo, nkgo,
Nkgo, nkgo,
Nkgo, nkgo,
nkgo, vul'em-nyan-go shu, shu, shu ku-ya-ba-nda. Nkgo, nkgo, nkgo, vul'em-nyan-go shu, shu,
nkgo, vul'em-nyan-go shu, shu, shu ku-ya-ba-nda. Nkgo, nkgo, nkgo, vul'em-nyan-go shu, shu,
nkgo, vul'em-nyan-go shu, shu, shu ku-ya-ba-nda. Nkgo, nkgo, nkgo, vul'em-nyan-go shu, shu,
nkgo, vul'em-nyan-go shu, shu, shu ku-ya-ba-nda. Nkgo, nkgo, nkgo, vul'em-nyan-go shu, shu,

shu, ku-ya-ba-nda. Yi-tsho-ni no-nke,____ yi-tsho-ni no-
shu, ku-ya-ba-nda. E - we, no-
shu, ku-ya-ba-nda. E - we, no-
shu, ku-ya-ba-nda. E - we, no-
nke si-ga-le-le-ki-le. Yi-tsho-ni no-nke,____ yi-tsho-ni no-
nke si-ga-le-le-ki-le. E - we, no-
nke si-ga-le-le-ki-le. E - we, no-
nke si-ga-le-le-ki-le. E - we, no-

nke si - ga - le - le - ki - le. Nkgo, nkgo, nkgo. Nkgo, nkgo,
nke si - ga - le - le - ki - le. Nkgo, nkgo, nkgo. Nkgo, nkgo,
nke si - ga - le - le - ki - le. Nkgo, nkgo, nkgo. Nkgo, nkgo,
nke si - ga - le - le - ki - le. Nkgo, nkgo, nkgo. Nkgo, nkgo,
nkgo. Nkgo, nkgo, nkgo, vul' em - nyan - go shu, shu,
nkgo. Nkgo, nkgo, nkgo, vul' em - nyan - go shu, shu,
nkgo. Nkgo, nkgo, nkgo, vul' em - nyan - go shu, shu,
nkgo. Nkgo, nkgo, nkgo, vul' em - nyan - go shu, shu,
To Coda
To Coda

CHORAL FOLK SONGS FROM SOUTH AFRICA

door, the wind blows cold. Knock, knock, knock, oh, please come o - pen the
door, the wind blows cold. Knock, knock, knock, oh, please come o - pen the
door, the wind blows cold. Knock, knock, knock, oh, please come o - pen the
door, the wind blows cold. Knock, knock, knock, oh, please come o - pen the
door, the wind blows cold. Come o - pen the door, come o - pen the
door, the wind blows cold. O - pen the
door, the wind blows cold. O - pen the
door, the wind blows cold. O - pen the

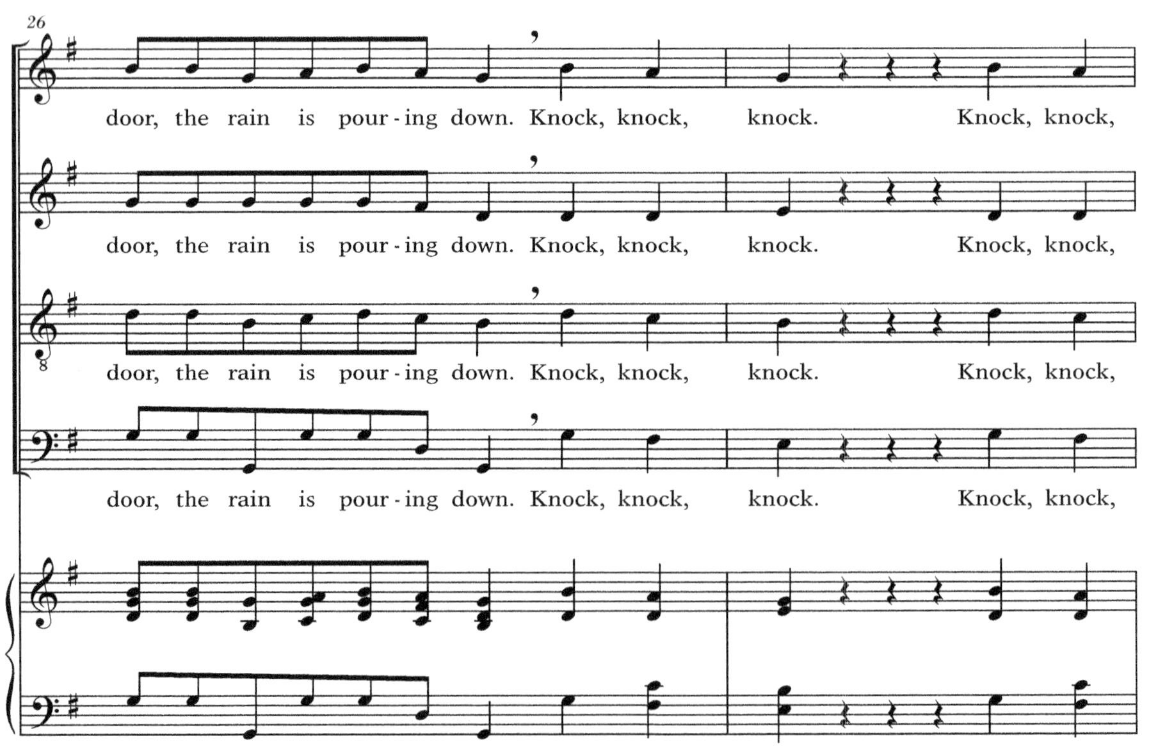

CHORAL FOLK SONGS FROM SOUTH AFRICA

28
knock. Knock, knock, knock, oh, won't you o - pen the
knock. Knock, knock, knock, oh, won't you o - pen the
knock. Knock, knock, knock, oh, won't you o - pen the
knock. Knock, knock, knock, oh, won't you o - pen the
30
door, the wind blows cold. Nkgo, nkgo,
door, the wind blows cold. Nkgo, nkgo,
door, the wind blows cold.
door, the wind blows cold.
D.S. al Coda
32 CODA
shu ku-ya - ba - nda.
shu ku-ya - ba - nda.
shu ku-ya - ba - nda.
shu ku-ya - ba - nda.
CODA

12. BABEVUYA
Wedding Song

It is customary for the bride to only show sadness during the wedding ceremony. When her party is ready to depart for the wedding, this song is sung to express this ceremonial sadness. It asserts that they were glad and rejoiced when the bridegroom brought the dowry, but today they are full of sadness... sadness like the bitterness of aloes.

A literal translation of the words would be: *They were jolly, they were singing and making music, but today the fist is sounding* (as in fighting). *Sons of my father, sons of my father, sons of my father, today the fist is sounding.*

How can this possibly be translated so that all the original meaning is clear to non-Africans? Obviously the solution is to sing the original words, which are quite simple, and enjoy the song for its fine melody, rich harmony, and interesting counter-rhythms. The basses sing in 3/4 time while the others sing in 6/8 time. You may want to try an accompaniment in 12/8 time, which will rhythmically result in a "two-against-three-against-four" feel.

The key of the original African transcription has been changed from A-flat to E-flat, necessitating slight changes in the bass part, and the switching of the alto and tenor parts.

Babevuya betshayalela kodwana mhlanje yincind'ye khala
Babevuya betshayalela kodwana mhlanje yincind'ye khala
'Ntoz'ka bawo, 'ntoz'ko bawo, 'ntoz'ka bawo yincind'ye khala
'Ntoz'ka bawo, 'ntoz'ko bawo, 'ntoz'ka bawo yincind'ye khala

PRONUNCIATION:
a as in *father*
e as in *egg*
o as in *obey*

12. BABEVUYA
Wedding Song

CHORAL FOLK SONGS FROM SOUTH AFRICA

48
8
Bb7
1. Eb
2. Eb
ba - wo,___ yin-cin-d'ye kha - la.___ 'Nto-z'ka kha - la. Ba-be-
ba - wo,___ yin-cin-d'ye kha - la.___ 'Nto-z'ka kha - la. Ba-be-
ha ho,___ ha ha ho,___ ha ha ho.___ Ba-be-
ha ho,___ ha ha ho,___ ha ha ho.___ Ba-be-
Bb7
1. Eb
2. Eb
11
Ab
Bb7
Eb
vu - ya be-tsha-ya - le - la___ ko-dwa-na mhlan - je___ yin-cin-d'ye kha - la.___
vu - ya be-tsha-ya - le - la___ mhlan - je___ yin-cin-d'ye kha - la.___
vu - ya be-tsha-ya - le - la___ ko-dwa-na mhlan - je___ yin-cin-d'ye kha - la.___
vu - ya be-tsha-ya - le - la___ mhlan - je___ yin-cin-d'ye kha - la.___
Ab
Bb7
Eb

13. UT'HE WENA
Wedding Song

Christian hymns are often sung in the South African church on the day of a wedding. However, a number of traditional melodies are still used to which hymn words are set.

This song is usually sung during the signing of the register. The words, translated literally, mean: *You said, you said, O our Father, You who created people, You created two. They are male and female. You said the word which still stands today. Let the man cleave to his wife and children.*

The lower voices sing syllables. They have no particular meaning, but are simply a musical accompaniment.

Ut'he wena, ut'he wena, bawo wet'hu
Ukuda la Bantu kwakho
Wabadala, wabadala bababini
Ba yindoda nenkazana
Walit'het'ha ne lo li zwi lisemiyo
Kwana namhlanje
Umntu maka, umntu maka shiy'n yi se
A manyane nomfaz' wakhe

It is written, it is written, I have seen it,
That we two should be as one.
And no matter, and no matter what befalls us
So may it be till life is done.
Through sickness and health,
Through hardship or wealth,
Whether for better or worse, we will be
Together, yes together, for the future,
And for the tasks that wait you and me.

PRONUNCIATION:
t'h is a cross between *t* and *th*
u as in *lute*
e as in *egg*
a as in *father*
o as in *obey*
kh as the *ch* in *Bach*

13. UT'HE WENA
Wedding Song

CHORAL FOLK SONGS FROM SOUTH AFRICA

10
Bb   C7   F
da - la ba - ba - bi - ni, Ba yin-do - da ne - nka - za__ na.
mat-ter what be - falls us So may it be till life is__ done.
ba - la - la - la, a - me-ni-za ba-la-la, a - me-ni-za ba-la-la, a-me-ni,
ba - la - la - la, la,__ ba-la - la, ba-la-la, a-me-ni,
ba - la - la - la, a-me-ni - za ba-la-la, a-me-ni - za ba-la-la, a-me-ni-za
Bb   C7   F
16
Wa - li - t'he__ t'ha ne__ lo li__ zwi li-se-mi-
Through__ sick - ness and health, Through__ hard - ship or wealth, wheth-er for
Bb
a - me - ni, a - me-ni-za ba-la - la, a - me-ni - za ba - la - la,
a - me - ni, a - me - ni, a - me - ni, a - me - ni, a - me - ni,
ba-la - la, a - me-ni-za ba-la-la, a - me-ni a - me-ni
Bb

yo Kwa-na, nam-hla-nje Um-ntu ma-ka, um-ntu ma-ka shi-y'n
bet-ter or worse, we will be to-geth-er, yes, to-geth-er for the

a-me-ni-za ba-la-la, a-me-ni-za ba-la-la, a-me-ni-za ba-la-la,

a-me-ni, a-me-ni, a-me-ni, a-me-ni, Ii - za ba-la-la-la,

a-me-ni - za ba-la-la, a-me-ni-za ba-la-la, a-me-ni-za ba-la-la-la,

yi - se A man-ya - ne no - mfaz' wa - khe.
fu - ture, And for the tasks that wait you and me.

a-me-ni-za ba-la-la, a-me-ni-za ba-la-la, a-me-ni.

la, ba-la - la, a-me-ni a-me-ni.

a-me-ni - za ba-la-la, a-me-ni - za ba-la-la, a-me-ni-za ba-la-la.

14. ISILEYI SAM
Wedding Song

This wedding song is sung during the daytime competitions, usually at home, though it has been heard during the night after the ceremony.

Some people may not call this musical fragment a song. Yet, it is extraordinary how it will take hold of a group that starts to sing it. Repeated over and over, it reminds one of a jeweler polishing a stone until it attains perfect luster and all its facets are brought out.

The literal meaning of the words is: *My heart melted with joy, my heart melted with joy.* Actually, these English words fit the melody rather well… but not as well, let us admit, as the African words. One wonders what would happen if other phrases appropriate to a wedding were applied to the notes, such as:

After all is said and done, you know that two can live as cheap as one.

A second verse in the original transcription has been omitted:

Yiza ne zembe ndingawule, meaning: *Bring that chopper, let me chop this.*

Like other songs in this collection, this composition can easily be taught by rote to a group of amateurs. One part after another is gradually added until all four mesh easily.

Satiyibilik Isileyi sam
Satiyibilik Isileyi sam

PRONUNCIATION:
a as in *father*
i like *ee*
e as in *egg*

14. ISILEYI SAM
Wedding Song

15. FATHER, FATHER, GOODBYE
Wedding Song

This song is normally sung after the wedding ceremony, just before the bride's departure from her own home and arrival to her new home with the bridegroom's family. Literally translated, the words mean: *You (my husband) are making me leave my parents.*

Using this phrase as a springboard, new lyrics have been created which, we hope, do not do too much violence to the original feeling. The African words, as you may see below, are difficult to pronounce and include many clicking noises.

Father, father, goodbye; and farewell, mother,
Father, father, goodbye; and farewell, mother,
I leave you now to begin with another,
I leave you now to begin with another,

I don't know how to give my feelings when I sing in the morning,
I don't know how to give my feelings when I sing in the morning,
La la la la, la-la-la, la la la la la,
La la la-la, la la, la la, la la la la la.

I leave you now to go off with my husband,
I leave you now to go off with my husband.

Undi shiyi sa baza linje yak'ndi gcina na kodwa
Undi shiyi sa baza linje yak'ndi gcina na kodwa
Nke wunkini yak'ndi gcina na kodwa
Nke wunkini yak'ndi gcina na kodwa

PRONUNCIATION:
u like the *oo* in *look*
i like *ee*
a as in *father*
e as in *egg*

The letters *gc* represent a click made by pulling the tongue down from the back of the roof of the mouth – a sound that can be difficult to achieve, especially in the middle of a word.

15. FATHER, FATHER, GOODBYE
Wedding Song

CHORAL FOLK SONGS FROM SOUTH AFRICA

leave you now to be - gin with an - oth - er. I
fare - well, moth - er. I leave you now to be -
fa - ther, good - bye; and fare - well, moth - er. I
gin with an - oth - er. I leave you now to be -
leave you now to be - gin with an - oth - er. I don't know
gin with an - oth - er. I leave you now to be -
leave you now to be - gin with an - oth - er. I
gin with an - oth - er. I leave you now to be -

how to give my feel-ings when I sing in the morn-ing. I don't know
gin with an-oth-er. I don't know how to give my feel-ings when I
leave you now to be-gin with an-oth-er. I don't know
gin with an-oth-er. I leave you now to be-
how to give my feel-ings when I sing in the morn-ing. La
sing in the morn-ing. I don't know how to give my feel-ings when I
how to give my feel-ings when I sing in the morn-ing. I don't know
gin with an-oth-er. I leave you now to be-

13
C7   F   B♭   F
la   la   la___   la   la   la   la   la   la   la___   la   la
sing   in   the   morn - ing.   La   la   la   la___   la   la   la
how   to   give   my   feel - ings   when   I   sing   in   the   morn - ing.   La
gin   with   an - oth - er.   I   leave   you   now___   to   be -
C7   F   B♭   F

15
C7   F   B♭   F
la   la   la   la   la___   la   la   la   la   la   la   la___   la.___
la   la   la   la___   la   la   la   la   la   la   la___   la   la   la
la   la   la   la   la   la   la   la   la   la___   la   la
gin   with   an - oth - er.   I   leave   you   now___   to   go
C7   F   B♭   F

CHORAL FOLK SONGS FROM SOUTH AFRICA

16. HEY, MOTSWALA
Wedding Song

This is a Sutho marriage song sung during the general festivities after the ceremony is over. The words, literally translated, mean: *O, my cousin, O, my cousin. My aunt has gone to Pretoria, she has run away from the iron spanner wrench (of a bicycle). I stamped and even sighed.*

A free translation to English is provided below.

The melody of the verse was sung as a New York City radio commercial in the 1940s. The melody was at that time thought to have come from Latin America. Who created it first? Perhaps we will never know.

The arrangement given here is slightly different from that transcribed in South Africa. It was learned from Mr. Henry Ramaila, of Zulu background.

Hey motswala, hey, motswala,
Hey motswala, hey, motswala,

FREE TRANSLATION:
My mother traveled to Pretoria
To sign the license for the wedding day.

Her father wants to give the bride away,
I think he's waiting for the dowry.

And now the time has come, I have to go,
I wish perhaps I hadn't hurried so.

16. HEY, MOTSWALA

Wedding Song

CHORAL FOLK SONGS FROM SOUTH AFRICA

13
A7
moth - er trav - eled to Pre - tor - i - a____ To sign the li - cense for the
moth - er trav - eled to Pre - tor - i - a____ To sign the li - cense for the
A7
16
D
A7
D
wed - ding day. Hey, mots - wa - la, hey, mots - wa - la,
wed - ding day. Hey, mots - wa - la, hey, mots - wa - la,
A - li - weh,____ a - li - weh,____
D
A7
D
21
A7
D
hey, mots - wa - la, hey, mots - wa - la.
hey, mots - wa - la, hey, mots - wa - la.
____ a - li - weh,____ a - li - weh.
A7
D

17. HERE'S TO THE COUPLE
Wedding Song

This wedding "competition" song is usually sung during the night, following the wedding, or during the signing of the register at church. Although some will say that it does not sound very African, the arrangement given here is note for note as transcribed from the singing of the African students mentioned in the foreword. Only an awkward bass solo, used as an introduction for the original arrangement, has been omitted.

The English words, however, are completely new, and bear no relation to the African words, as you will see by the literal translation given below. At time of writing a number of American couples have been married to its accompaniment.

Lo mfan' unesangota
Lo mfan' unesangota
Ha dovale le ma gqibelaka Nkqo yi
Ndi khokele O Yehova
Nginumhambi nkosi yami
Una mandla a ndi na wo
Ebu that ha ke ni bami
O msindi si, O msindi si
Nguwe O li khakala me

PARTIAL LITERAL TRANSLATION:
This boy has guts.
Save me, O Jehovah,
I am a pilgrim, my Lord.
Thou are almighty
I have it in my misery.

17. HERE'S TO THE COUPLE
Wedding Song

CHORAL FOLK SONGS FROM SOUTH AFRICA

To Coda
for - tune and health of the best, We wish them good for - tune and
teach - er and make all the rules, Let love be the teach - er and
for - tune and health of the best, Wish them good for - tune and
teach - er and make all the rules, Love be the teach - er and
for - tune and health of the best, Wish them good for - tune and
teach - er and make all the rules, Love be the teach - er and
for - tune and health of the best, Wish them good for - tune and
teach - er and make all the rules, Love be the teach - er and
health of the best, Strong chil - dren, good neigh-bors and all the
make all the rules, Let love be the doc - tor and cure the
health of the best, Al - so good neigh - bors and all the
make all the rules, Love be the doc - tor and cure the
health of the best. And al - so have good neigh-bors and all the
make all the rules, Re - mem - ber, Love be the doc - tor and cure the
health of the best, Al - so good neigh - bors and all the
make all the rules, Love be the doc - tor and cure the
To Coda

CHORAL FOLK SONGS FROM SOUTH AFRICA

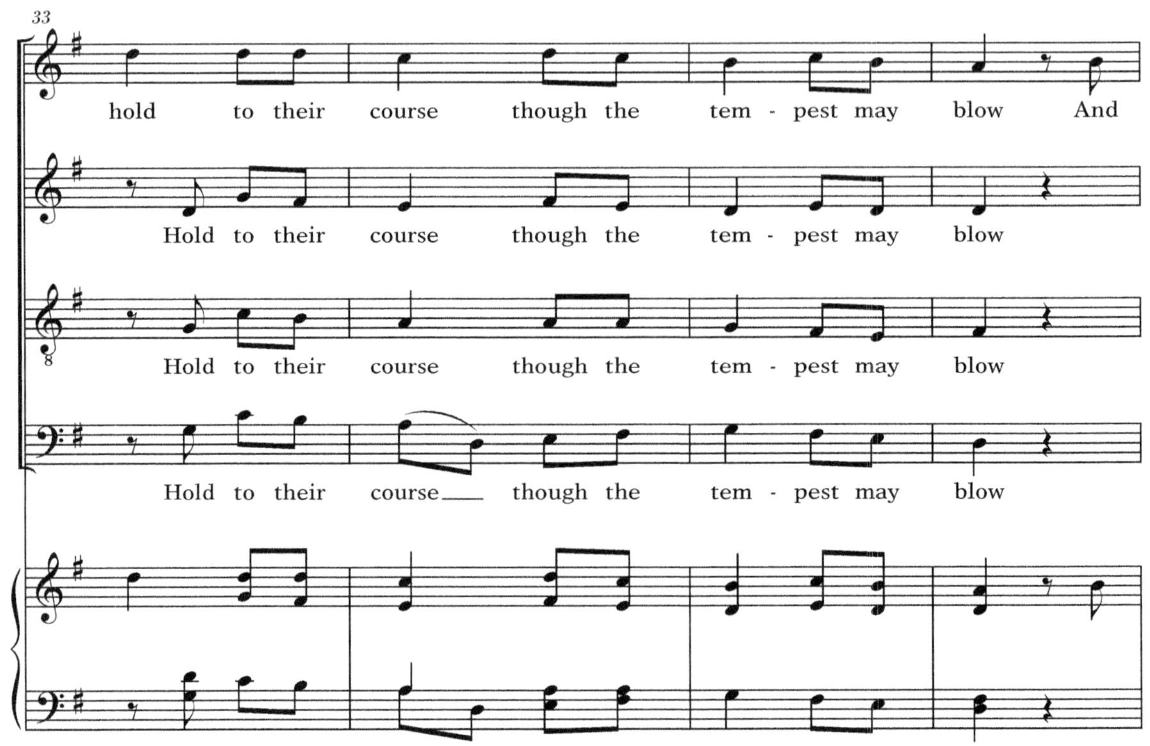

hold to their course be it north, south or east. May they
hold to their course be it north, south or east.
hold to their course be it north, south or east.
Hold to their course be it north, south or east.
hold to their course though the tem - pest may blow And
Hold to their course though the tem - pest may blow
Hold to their course though the tem - pest may blow
Hold to their course though the tem - pest may blow

reach their goal, the goal of us all: For
And reach their goal, the goal of us all:
And reach their goal, the goal of us all for-ev-er:
And reach their goal, the goal of us all:
them and their chil-dren, a world at peace, For
And for their chil-dren, a world at peace,
And their chil-dren, a world at peace for ev-er,
And for their chil-dren, a world at peace,

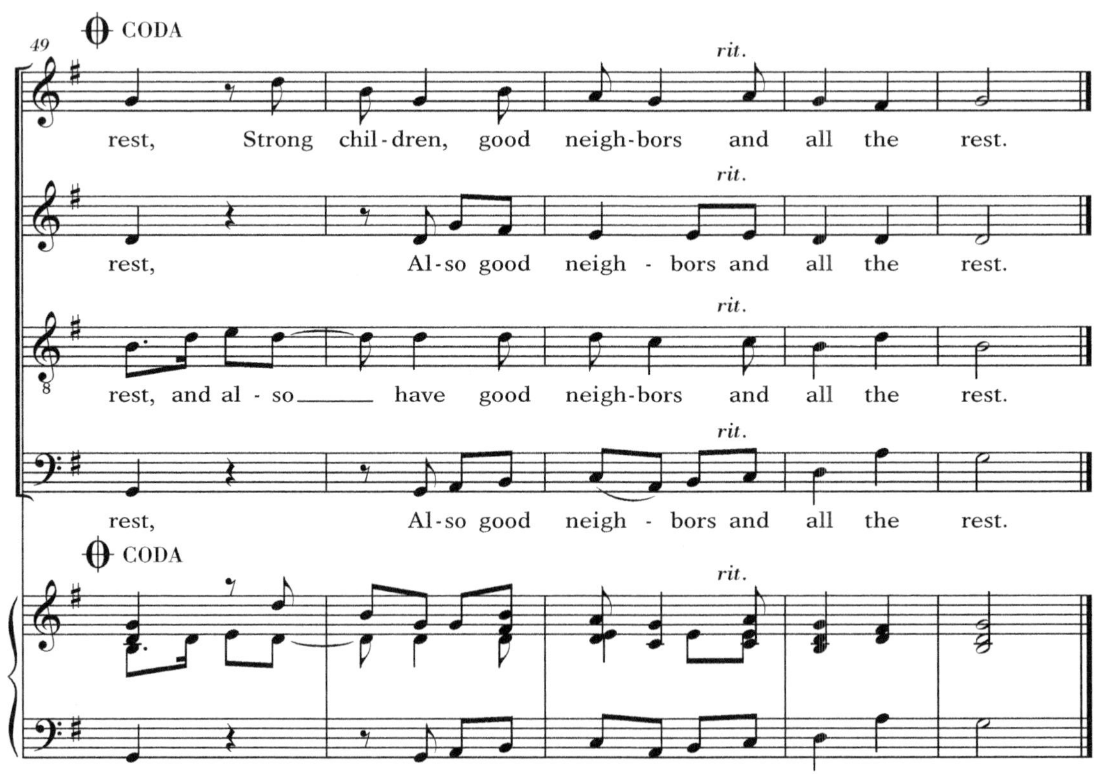

CHORAL FOLK SONGS FROM SOUTH AFRICA

MISCELLANEOUS SONGS

18. UQONGQOT'HWANE
Children's Song

This song poses an intriguing linguistic problem. The title word has two "clicks" in it, sounds made by pulling the tongue down from the roof of the mouth. It is difficult to make these sounds while pronouncing other consonants and vowels, but it can be done with practice.

This song adheres to traditional parallel harmonization, a type of harmony popular in parts of South Africa. The small boys herding cattle or sheep often sing this song when they hunt for a beetle called Uqongqot'hwane. If they catch him, they can make him dance when they sing this song.

Igquira lendlela Nguqongqot'hwane.
Igquira lendlela Nguqongqot'hwane.
Ube qubele gqi th'apha Uqongqot'hwane,
Ube qubele gqi th'apha Uqongqot'hwane.

Oh, catch him, oh, grab him, Uqongqot'hwane,
Oh, catch him, oh, grab him, Uqongqot'hwane.

Won't you dance for us, Doctor Uqongqot'hwane,
Won't you dance for us, Doctor Uqongqot'hwane?

On a hot and dusty road lies Uqongqot'hwane,
On a hot and dusty road lies Uqongqot'hwane.

Oh, tricky one, Oh, Doctor Uqongqot'hwane,
Oh, tricky one, Oh, Doctor Uqongqot'hwane.

PRONUNCIATION:
q represents a click (see above)
i like *ee*
u as in *lute*
e as in *egg*
a as in *father*

T'h is pronounced halfway between *t* and *th*, thus *t'hwane* sounds faintly like *twahnay.*

18. UQONGQOT'HWANE
Children's Song

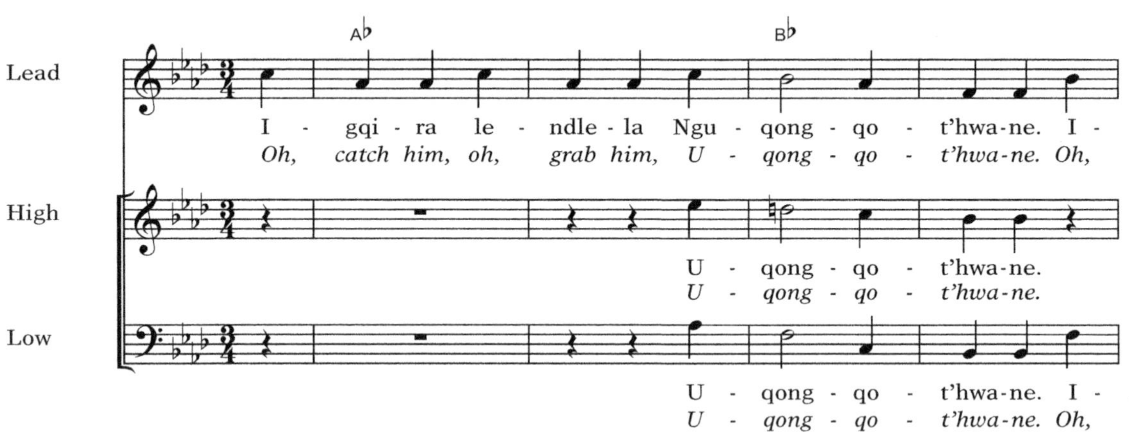

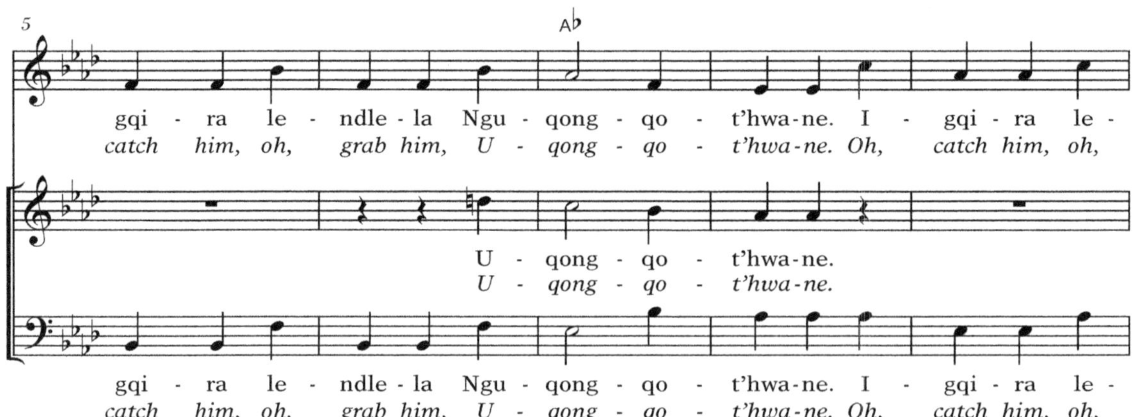

If needed, the high and low vocal lines may be used as a piano accompaniment.

CHORAL FOLK SONGS FROM SOUTH AFRICA

CHORAL FOLK SONGS FROM SOUTH AFRICA

19. ICAMAGU

This song is used to "warm up" the shaman during the process of divining. It is normally punctuated by a high descant or imprecations added by the shaman.

Icamagu limkile Malibuyel'ekhaya yo ho
Wohayo limkile
Wohayo lifikile
Mdew'yase gqile yo ho

PARTIAL TRANSLATION:
iCamgau (or Icamagu) – a traditional healer who propitiates ancestral spirits
limkile – it/he/she (the traditional healer) has departed
Malibuye – let it/him/her return
ekhaya – to home
lifikili – it/he/she has arrived

19. ICAMAGU

div.
Tenor
Baritone
Bass
Piano
(for rehearsal
purposes only)
Ma-li-bu yel' e-kha-ya,
I - ca-ma-gu li - mki - le   Ma-li-bu yel' e-kha-ya,
Ma-li-bu yel' e-kha-ya,

Ma-li-bu yel' e-kha-ya,   Yo - ho.   Ma-li-bu yel' e-kha-ya,
Ma-li-bu yel' e-kha,   I - ca-ma-gu li - mki - le   Ma-li-bu yel' e-kha-ya,
Ma-li-bu yel' e-kha-ya,   Yo.   Ma-li-bu yel' e-kha-ya,

Ma-li-bu yel' e-kha-ya. Ma-li-bu yel' e-kha-ya,
Ma-li-bu yel' wo-ha-yo li-mki-le Ma-li-bu yel' e-kha-ya,
Ma-li-bu yel' e-kha-ya. Ma-li-bu yel' e-kha-ya,
Ma-li-bu yel' e-kha-ya, Yo-ho. Ma-li-bu yel' e-kha-ya,
Ma-li-bu yel' wo-ha-yo li-fi-ki-le Ma-li-bu yel' e-kha-ya,
Ma-li-bu yel' e-kha-ya, Yo. Ma-li-bu yel' e-kha-ya,
Ma-li-bu yel' e-kha-ya, Yo-ho. Mbew' ya-se-gqi-li, Mbew' ya-
Ma-li-bu yel' e-kha, U-mgwa-dla-nyan' Mbew' ya-se-gqi-li, Mbew' ya-
Ma-li-bu yel' e-kha-ya, Yo. Mbew' ya-se-gqi-li, Mbew' ya-

se - gqi - li, Mbew' ya - se-gqi - li, Mbew' ya - se-gqi -
se-gqil' Um-gwad-la-nya-ni Mbew' ya-se-gqi-li, Mbew' ya-se-gqi. Um-
se-gqi - li, Mbew' ya - se-gqi - li, Mbew' ya - se-gqi -
li, Mbew' ya - se-gqi-li, Mbew' ya - se-gqi - li,
gwad-la-nya-ni Mbew' ya - se-gqi-li, Mbew' ya - se-gqi. Um-gwad-la-nya-ni
li, Mbew' ya - se-gqi-li, Mbew' ya - se-gqi - li,
yo.
Mbew' ya - se-gqi - li, Mbew' ya - se-gqi - li, yo-ho.
Mbew' ya - se-gqi - li, Mbew' ya - se-gqi - li, yo-ho.
Mbew' ya - se-gqi - li, Mbew' ya - se-gqi - li, yo.

20. SENZENNINA

Until now all the songs in this book have been old village songs, but we thought it would be appropriate to include one of the many songs sung in the long struggle for democracy. As result of a worldwide boycott of South Africa in the 1980s, the era of apartheid ended and Nelson Mandela was elected President in 1994.

This song has only one word in it. It means: *What have we done,* repeated over and over and over. Obvious answer: we were born with dark skins. This song became famous when it was sung by several hundred women who, with careful planning, strolled from different directions into a residential square in a wealthy white neighborhood. They sang this song over and over again with ever richer harmony, until finally the police came and ordered them all to disperse.

20. SENZENNINA

Freedom Song

Author unknown
ca. 1955?

Arranged by Pete Seeger

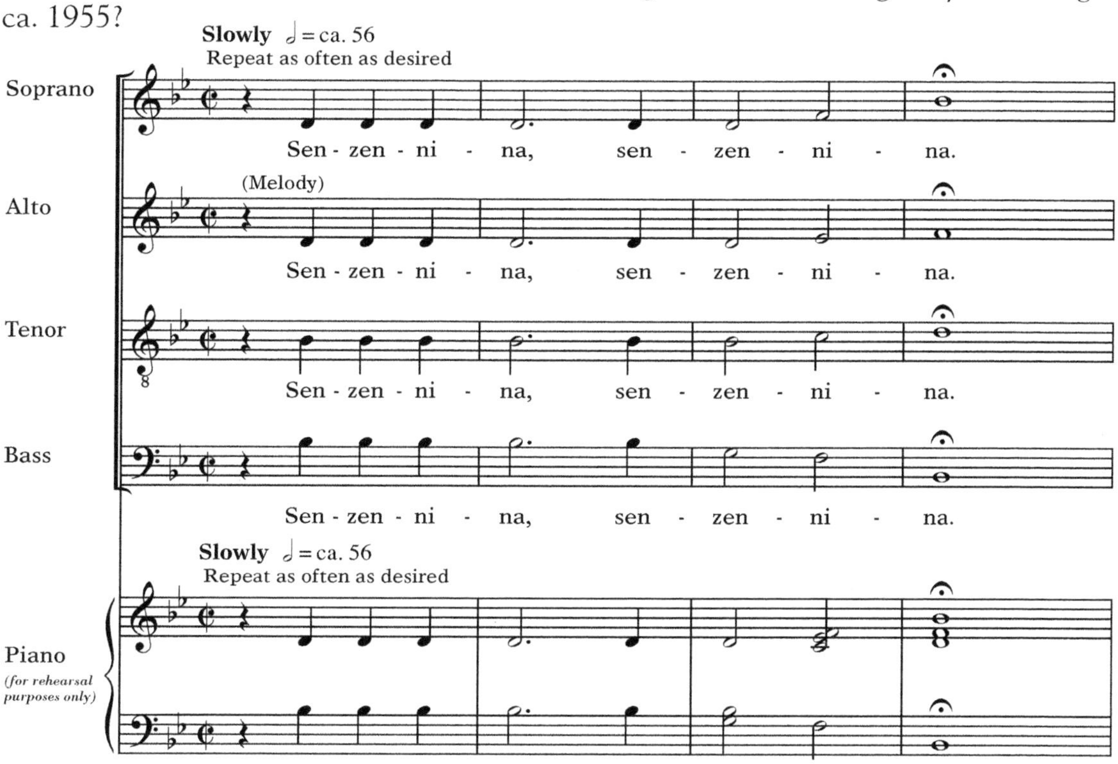

Some 1st tenors could sing the melody with the altos.

CHORAL FOLK SONGS FROM SOUTH AFRICA

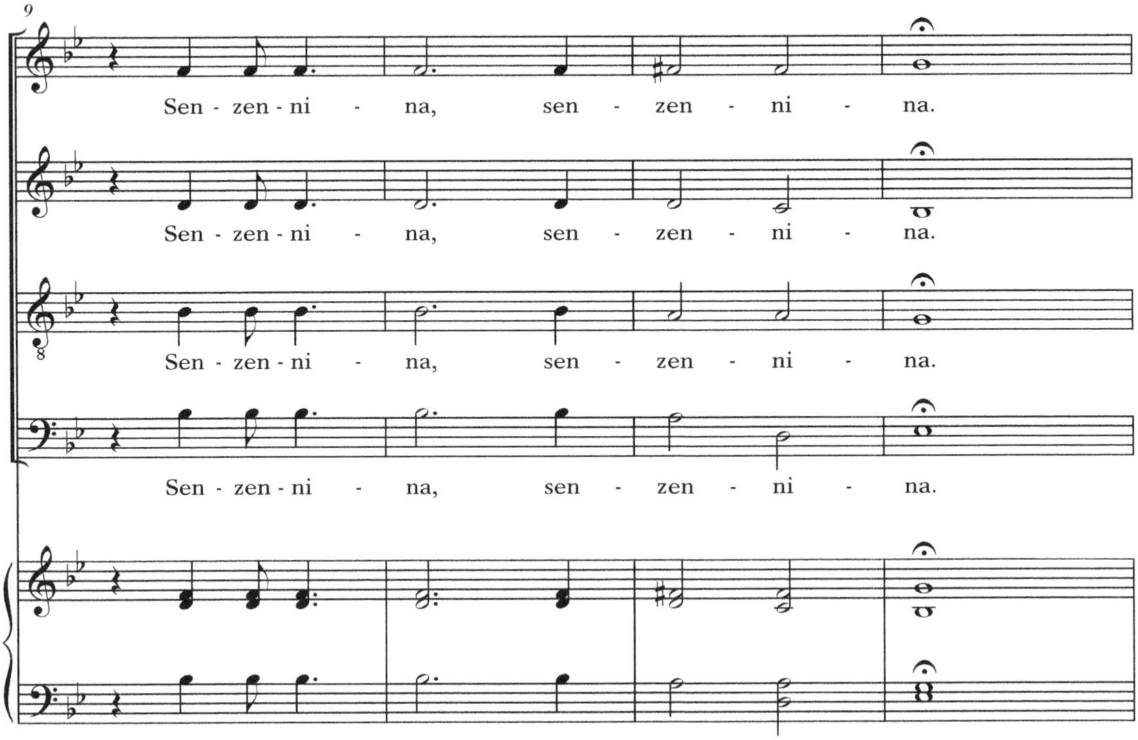

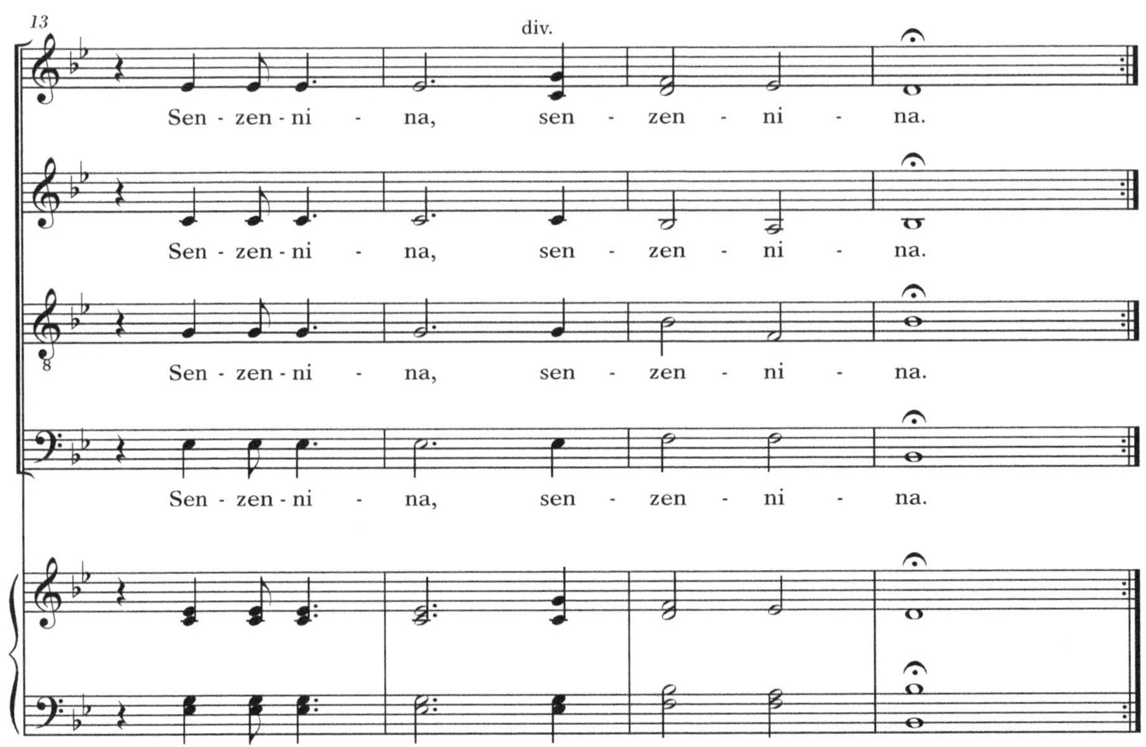

CHORAL FOLK SONGS FROM SOUTH AFRICA